EMPRESS

JuJu Ave: Where Black Girl Magic & Magic in General Reside

A Beginner's to Intermediate Guide to Finding and Crafting your Magical Path

Contents

JuJu Foreword

JuJu is energy, an energy that is readily available to everyone willing to tap into it. It's up to you to choose your path.

Conjure is not Hoodoo or Voodoo or Santeria, it is a culmination of traditions, energy and knowledge stemmed respectfully from cultures and laws that have been around since the beginning of human kind. It is the acknowledgement of the ability to exercise one's free will.

JuJu is doing your research and your spiritual work and findng what resonates within you the most.

You are an energetic being and therefore, obliged and naturally encouraged and welcome to interact with the energy around you.

You do not have to subscribe to a particular Deity or religion to impress your will and intention upon the Universal energy that is. Regardless of if you ever harvest an herb, consult with the tarot or call upon the specific deities, the energy is absolute and readily awaiting for you to interact.

Many people shy away from God given rights and gifts due to fear, but the truth is, there is nothing to be afraid of.The energy will remain present whether you engage in it or not. It's up to you to decide whether the Earth's gifts are delighting to your senses.

A key to divination, conjure and magic in general is releasing fear and letting go of preconceived notions, especially those related to fear. Allowing your spirit to lead and guide will help you discern with the the spiritual realm as you do the physical. If something doesn't feel right, end the connection. You are not obligated to interact with anyone or anything!!

Many things are double edged, be knowledgeable and firm before you go running head first in to a seance, summoning random spirits and invoking energies you have no connection to or knowledge of. Just as you can put yourself in danger venturing into dark places where you are unsure, unknown or unrepresented, the same is true of the spiritual realm.

There are many sides and angles in conjure and magic and many ways to manifest using the light side of the game. There is a universal energy of gratitude to be tapped into, the elements of the Universe (water, air, fire, earth) can be called into play and spiritual allies such as ancestors (especially those that really had your back when they were on the physical realm). It's perfectly fine to start small, to conquer your ego and fears and to understand the vessel you operate before you open yourself to others. Starting with self care and self love and understanding will start you on an invaluable foundation.

Practice with respect and caution and you will be fine. Research and read, walk humbly but confidently as you approach, and if you decide to join "ranks,"(entity magic, invocations, necromancy, deity rituals), make sure you learn the "Chain of Command" because just like any other set of secular knowledge, there are rules to this shit! Bless up loves, and may you find balance in all things you do.

1

What's That Jar for?

Jars are another old school favorite. Working a jar is like dressing a candle but infusing it with energy over time. Its a heightened ritual using the almighty candle to assist the energy.

The jar is filled with herbs, crystals, petitions, pictures and other additives to intertwine and mingle while they work together in a confined space to manifest your intention. Usually, jars are set and then initially charged with a candle and possibly a second ritual. After charging the jar, the jar may be carried to

intensify the emitting aura and letting it surround and effect in your favor. This method is usually for jars like honey jars and sugar jars that are used to sweeten intentions, dispositions, situations and/or people. The jar can be carried or left on altar.

The jar can also be hidden and forgotten as an "out of sight out of mind" technique to allow the petition to manifest (business jars, wish jars, drawing goals). The jars can also be placed in the freezer to stop someone in their tracks, stop people from talking/gossiping, spreading gossip, harassing you or giving you a hard time, to "chill someone out." Sour jars, vinegar jars, banishing jars, return to sender jars etc...All can be discarded at the crossroads, a dump, dumpster and for the ultimate grounding, rooting and extension power, buried.

Decide what you need your jar for, once you have decided, write your intentions,preferably on parchment paper, but any unlined paper is fine. Really take your time to decide the herbs and/or items

that you will place into your jar to support your intention. Once the jar is sealed, its usually best to let it do its thing, if you would like to add something after ritual and sealing, I would recommend just creating a new jar. Place your items into your jar , herbs, petition, crystals, any small items related to intention, picture of self or other. Say a few words, pray over the jar, take a moment to sit with your jar and intention, light your candle on top of your jar, stay with it as long as you need and release.

If the jar is for someone else and you cant find a picture on either social media, or google image world, a name is fine, write the name on paper three to nine times or until you're satisfied.

It's perfectly fine to get creative with these jars, it should feel good and guided, just keep calm and follow your intuition.

COMMON ADDS FOR HONEY JAR

- Honey : ultimate sweetening and attraction agent
- Molasses : sweet, bonding long lasting, works take a little longer than honey but have deeper and longer lasting effects
- Agave: light love, playful
- Sugar: quick sweet results
- Rose: love Emitting
- Lovage: love drawing
- Jasmine : spiritual love, friendship, luxury

- Lavender: friendship and love cooperation
- Damiana: intensify sexual love/ sexual energy
- Hibiscus : Passion, lust, fiery sex energy
- Violet : wishes, healing after breakup, promotes faithfulness while in one
- Lilac : flirtation, new love, romance
- Orris root: love holding, encourages lasting love and relationships
- Jezebel Root: bending, commanding, wealthy suitor attraction, "tips" attraction; great for sex worker and service and commission workers
- Lemon Verbana: beauty and glamour, increase attractiveness
- Rose Hips: resonating love)
- Marigold(Calendula) : bright moods, happiness, platonic love, friendship
- Cinnamon : energy amp, attraction properties
- Cardamon: lustful love, passion attracting, love drawing, encourages eloquence
- Vanilla: lowering the guard, sweeten the infusion, rich love
- Blue Lotus: Goddess invocation, aura, euphoric feelings
- Honeysuckle: fun love light love, flirtation
- Star Anise : luck in love and money
- Periwinkle: lasting love
- Passion Flower : attracting friends and prosperity, increasing popularity, clinging love
- Parchment Paper
- Intentions

HONEY JARS

For sweetening aura, situations, others dispositions toward you, focusing love vibes, self love, relationship love, mending love, general aura sweetener

In all honesty, a honey jar can be made with only honey and a written petition; Adding herbs, oils, crystals are added for more specific intentions. Honey on its own
is a powerful sweetening and attracting agent.

Jars are completely up to you. You can keep it simple by placing a petition in honey, adding only rose and honey for sweet love, doing a sugar jar with sugar and petition for quick sweet results. It's completely up to you how to craft your jar, follow your heart.

Here are a few jar your can start with, the ingredients are not set in stone, rather a guide to help you along the way.

STARTER HONEY JAR (aura sweetening, attracting loving vibes, bright vibes, favors, having people "sweet on you"

- Rose Petals
- Rose Hips
- Calendula(Marigold)
- Five Finger Grass
- Pinch of Jasmine
- Dash of coconut or Brown Sugar
- Mucho Honey

*Use a pink, yellow, red, or white candle

QUICK MONEY HONEY JAR Used to draw in a specific amount quickly. Can brought on by means of attraction, increased business, favorites Description)

- Pyrite and/or Money Rice
- "Apple Pie Spice" mix (Allspice, Nutmeg, Cinnamon)
- Clove
- Bay Leaf
- Basil
- Five Finger Grass
- Honey

*Optional pinch of Chamomile for luck
  **Switch honey for sugar for even faster results
  ***Use a green, gold, orange or white candle

LONG MONEY PROSPERITY JAR

- Pyrite
- Molasses
- Patchouli
- Saffron
- Jasmine Flowers
- Cedar
- Cloves
- "Apple Pie Spice" mix
- Dried orange peel or Sweet Orange essential oil

BOSS FIX JAR : To "fix" a boss at work. To thwart aggressiveness, pettiness and/or bullying behaviors of an overbearing boss; To Sweeten Boss more on you(for promotion, consideration), to get a authority figure to be less harsh and/or more favorable to you.

- High John the Conqueror Root : for conquering, ability to influence
- Calamus: bending, covers flaws
- Sugar : harmony
- Molasses : long lasting effect
- Kola Nut : encourages unity
- Bay Leaf : protection

*Optional Licorice for domination, mutual peace and under-standing. "Stay away from me i'll stay away from you)

**Burn black , blue, white candle on top and charge with a Black Tourmaline Crystal (crystal is optional but it is situation turning and protective.)

*Put in freezer and walk away.

COUPLES HONEY JAR : to mend or strengthen a love of two who want to be with each other but may be rocky or just to intensify feelings and emotions that are already there.

As with all things you can "do whatever you want" however, there is always balance in the law so there will always be an equal reaction to every other action. Practice with caution and do your best not to try and FORCE anyone to love you or be with you, if you do, go with caution.

Ingredients for Couple's Jar

- Honey : sweetness
- Molasses : longevity
- Rose : romantic love
- Hibiscus : passion
- Marigold : happiness , friendship
- Periwinkle : pleasure, faithfulness

- Orris Root : holds love, makes love last
- Yarrow : makes love last
- Rose Hips : bring love to equal accord
- Lavender : cooperation
- Damiana : intensify sexual love
- Coconut Sugar : quick healing, protection of bond
- Cinnamon Stick : Spice it up!
- Cardamom : passion, aphrodisiac
- Vanilla Bean: lowering guard, sweeten connection

*Light a pink, red or white candle on top of the jar preferably two dressed together with each of your names on a candle to represent the couple.

SOUR JARS

Sour jars are usually made to curse, to return a jinx, to break a bad habit, or for banishing and binding work.

Some let "Karma" make its way to people and some people take Karma into their own hands. To bypass hurting someone on the physical realm, sour jars allow you to exact your revenge in the spiritual realm and let it manifest on the physical plane.

These are items that can be added to sour jars, as always use caution when delving into any realm.

- Vinegar : souring, dissolves relationships, eats away
- Lemon : souring, reveals truth, burning, irritating
- Lime : souring, encourages deceit, irritatingVodka : freezing, makes the work last.
- Whiskey : makes bitter, makes the work last.

- Hot peppers (Cayenne, Chili Powder) : anger, hot foot, getting rid of , cause fighting
- Garlic : disgust and repulsion.
- Onion: disconnects relationships.
- Poppy seeds : confusion and intoxication (psychic attack)
- Alum : stops communication, dry mouth, gibbered speech.
- Small Cucumber Pickles : male impotency.
- Beet Pickles : female hormonal problems.
- Salt : painful cleansing, salt in the wound.
- Black pepper : revealing truth, blinding.
- Green Apples : unrequited love, deceit, promotes distrust, disagreements
- Radishes : sexual shame, Sexually Transmitted Disease(STD's)
- Cloves : domination
- Licorice Root : domination
- Ants : eat away happiness.
- Scorpions : sting, cause betrayal
- Spider : danger, complicated trouble, inflict anxiety
- Bees : punishment, stinging
- Flies : irritate and annoy, constant irritation
- Wasp : heavy Stings, Head on confrontation
- Broken glass : cut ties, emotional wounds
- Pins : many small pains, cause agony
- Thumbtacks : make the work stick in them
- Razor blades : sadistic actions, sharp words
- Needles : Use with caution, very binding agent
- Rusty Nails : disintegrate, cause sickness
- Grave Dirt : enlists the help of a spirit or spirits for your goal.
- Grave dirt: is dirt secured from a specific plot (You want to

rob a bank, an infamous, successful,bank robber has a plot near you, you may use dirt from his plot for a success and protection ritual/jar.)
· Graveyard Dirt : to cause death, torment. Graveyard dirt is taken from the general graveyard area, not a specific plot but land surrounding plots.

*It is customary, traditional and highly recommended (in almost every form of magic that I know) to at the very least leave offerings for taking from the graveyard in general and also to specific spirits or taking from their plot. An offering can be left at the gate of the graveyard to appease the spirits and energy and specific offering can be left at grave site.

**Common offerings include candy, fruit, flowers, goodies, toys, cigarettes, cigars, alcohol.

Put it in a jar! I keep them in my house, on my altar, under my altar, I use small jars to carry and to hang on my rear view mirror, my blind pullers, my neck, a good jar can fix anything!

2

Witches' Brewery

MAGICKAL BREWERY

The Brewery is about herbal drink concoctions! Getting lifted, centered or both turns regular "tea time" into magic.

As with all things, make these drinks with intention, while preparing the herbs as you are mixing brewing them. Hold that intention while drinking, clearly visualize your manifestation and drink with joy and the feeling that all that you desire is already yours! Make it a ritual to drink your herbs daily, tea is perfect at any time of the day or night and the herbs are working 24/7 so anytime you can think of "Mood Magic" you can enhance or heal in the brewery.

Drinking herbs is both magically and physically healing. Herbs have regenerative and uplifting properties that when incorporated into your daily routine represents a clear and purposeful act of self care and love. Ingesting herbs is akin to drinking and eating your medicine.

"SUNSHINE" LEMON GINGER

- Lemon Balm
- Squeezed Lemon
- Fresh Ginger
- Calendula
- Honey
- (served hot or cold, brew herbs, squeeze in lemon or brew with lemon slices)
- Mood Boosting
- Refreshing
- Skin Brightening
- Overall Aura Uplift

Visualize the perfect sunrise lightly shining on you, comforting you, increasing your light and giving you vitality.

"BED OF FLOWERS"(Relaxation Tea)

For when you want to fall back into a bed of flowers, soft floral notes, with full tones of mint and zest . Relax and imagine yourself surrounded by soft, flourishing (non allergenic flowers) calming floral blend with a minty zing.

- Rose/Lemon or Bee Balm
- Nice lunch of Lemon Verbana
- Lavender
- Damiana
- Mint
- Marjoram

"LOVE ME DOWN" HONEY JAR TEA

For promoting self love and sweetening your aura, a sweet, endearing blend to encourage an intense loving vibe. For the heart and core, love and passion, general happiness and an inviting vibe.

- Rose Hips
- Rose
- Hibiscus
- Calendula
- Chamomile
- Honey

NIGHT CAP WITH THE QUEEN

An aphrodisiac blend, promoting soulful connection and an exhilarating, euphoric vibe. Use for a seductive night, a blend to stimulate the spiritual attraction involved with Goddess energy. Third Eye level Sex Magic

- Blue Lotus
- Red Wine
- Cardamon
- Ginger

*Can also be made as tea with honey minus the red wine

CLEAR SKIES, SWEET DREAMS (Sleepy-time Tea)

A mint version of Chai tea that can be used as ; a"sleepy-time" tea that gently relaxes you and allows you to remain active in your sleep. This tea promotes restful sleep, astral travel, lucid dreaming and clarity afterward.

- Marjoram
- Mugwort
- Damiana
- Skullcap
- Moringa
- Coconut Milk (can be replaced with milk of choice)
- Cinnamon
- Honey
- Raw Vanilla bean scraping

*Dash of ginger if you like the spice.

RICH LOVE & PASSION

An Aphrodisiac blend promotes fiery, passionate, rich sex. For a turn up night and abundant pleasure. For "celebration sex," sex magic, money magic.

- Hibiscus
- Rose Petals
- Jasmine
- Vetivert
- Cloves
- Cinnamon
- Allspice
- Star Anise

(*Drink as hot tea or drink on ice, for a more intense "turn up" night, add whiskey, bourbon, rum, cognac.

LUXURY & WEALTH ON ICE (Herbal Limeade)

For luxurious relaxation, taking the time to meditate on and manifest the wealth and luxury you imagine and enjoy in your life. When life gives you "limon", truly take a second to make "limonada."

- Lime Juice
- Honey, Agave, or Coconut Sugar
- Lavender
- Mint

**Garnish with Jasmine Flowers (optional)
  **Add Vodka, Ciroc orPatron to really heighten intention

KITCHEN HERBS

FOR COOKING

- Rosemary : protection
- Thyme : loyalty, affection, strength thru grief, good luck
- Basil : money, customer attraction
- Parsley : healing, money
- Allspice : money, Energizer
- Tumeric : protection, healing , promotes good health
- Ginger : prosperity, success, energizer, confidence booster, promotes sexuality
- Bay Leaf : money
- Cayenne Pepper : get rid of, spice up
- Chili Powder : hex breaking, love/lust
- Cloves : money, lust passion
- Cardamon : love drawing, lust

- Cinnamon : money, luck , incense, energizer
- Cumin : protection, banishing negative energy,promotes fidelity
- Dill : Evil Eye protection, money
- Garlic : evil repellent
- Oregano : joy, strength , additional energy, family love, closeness
- Salt : protection, banishment, equalizer

DRINKING HERBS & FLOWERS

- Mint : money drawing, mood boosting
- Lemon/Rose/Bee Balm : mood brightening, menstrual help
- Catnip : attracts men to women, woman's herb, menstrual help, luck and happiness
- Marjoram : restore optimism, thwarts sadness and grief, uplifting
- Rose : love
- Rose Hips : holds love together
- Hibiscus : passion, lust, sex magic
- Lavender : peace, calm, tranquility, clarity
- Irish Moss : financial abundance, great luck, business success
- Calendula : happiness, friendship
- Carnation : protection, strength, healing
- Chamomile : luck attracting, energizer, success
- Orange Peel : attraction, abundance
- Lemongrass : magical skill developing
- Lemon : clearing blockages, cleansing, digestive help

- Spearmint : strength, money, healing
- Mullein : protection from nightmares, promotes comfortable sleep

EXTRAS :

- Aloe Vera : protection, relieves loneliness, health promoting
- Coconut (fruit, water, milk) : Protection
- Honey : sweetening, attracting
- Molasses : makes thing last

3

Light a Fire Baybee: A Chapter on Candles

Candles have been used since the beginning of time to light the way and to communicate with the spirit world.

Candles are an integral element of rituals, offerings and magic in general.

Votive candles, tealight candles, pillar candles and 7 day candles are the most common but any candle can be used.

The importance lies more in the color, the intention and the dressing of the candle.

Candles always incorporate the Fire element and are further incensed when adding Earth (herbs and crystals). Air element is invoked by smoke and water is always ideal to have around when lighting a candle, especially when communicating with the spirit world.

Candles should never be left burning unattended. However, if you choose to do so, an acceptable and safer way would be to place to the candle in a bowl of water.

Candles are my absolute favorite method of conjure. They can be used to manifest a petition, show gratitude, honor someone or for Divination. Candles work well because they give us something to leave our worries to. Burn and let go!

DRESSING CANDLES : For me, dressing candles is definitely a ritual in itself. The transfer of energy is immense. Focus all of your intention, energy and desires as you dress the candle. If you are using a "free standing" candle (candle not set in glass) for certain rituals it's proper to inscribe the candle by writing your name a number of the times to surround the candle, binding the candle to the named party (self or other). Using a pencil is fine for inscription unless you have a specific magical scribe you like to use. For candles set in glass, you may write the name directly on top.

Now, rub the candle down with oil(s) of choice, visualize and or vocalize your intent as you dress the candle with oil (Visualization and Intent are keys!). For candles set in glass dress the top and take a moment to acknowledge what you intend to manifest.

At this point you are ready for the herbs, for loose (candles not set in glass) you can add a little honey to sweeten the work and to more easily collect the herbs, roll out your herb/incense blend and lay the candles on top. Roll the candles in the blend, sprinkle a little more on top if you desire.

For glass set candles, dress the top as you did the oil and visualize your intention, you can also add honey here for sweetening effect.

Remember, it's more about the energy and intention than the look. However, a party is more enjoyable when the ambiance, theme and look of the place is inviting and correspond with the intention.

FLAME

Pay attention when using a candle in a spell.

Always trim your wick to about an half an inch or shorter and let the flame build itself up.

The flame speaks to you, the energy of the candle and even the way the wax melts and lands sends a message. It is a full work of energy in itself and full of information and communication. Since early times, candles have been used to illuminate and light the way "physically and metaphorically." Times have changed but some entities are simply timeless.

Flame communication can be elaborate in many ways but there are also common consensus on what certain movements and results mean.

A few common burns and meanings include:

A regular burning flame is always good news, a good consistent clean burn is ideal.

High Flickering flame usually denotes that there is high activity being made on your behalf and you should expect quick results.

Popping and Flickering denotes that the message has been received.

Low burning flame shows low chance of success. Pray over the candle and make sure your intention is crystal clear (as always candles are man made , if candle is burning

low make sure that the wick has not dropped over. If this is the case, allow the wax to cool, lift wick, trim to half an inch, pray over the candle and re-light .)

Dud candle means no for now, try again.

Sit with your candle as it burns for a while, watch the flame and how it changes, discern as much as possible. Reach and listen for communication that may not be as simple as high or low flickering flame.

For rituals and myself, if the candle isn't virtually a clean burn, I "re-specify," clarify, and make sure my intentions are clean cut and clear and start over with a new candle.

COLORS

RED: passion, rapid results, magic of flesh, sex magic, fiery love, strength, fiery energy, power, intensity, war

ORANGE : attraction, warm energy, balance, energy booster, abundance, uplifting energy

YELLOW : happiness, cleansing, refreshing energy, clarity, platonic relationships, friendships

GREEN : money, growth, healing, earth magic(offerings) Mostly and especially money magic

BLUE : tranquility, calm, ancestral (maternal, nurturing protection) ocean energy (air, water)

PURPLE : royalty, luxury, peace, sleep, spiritual awareness, mystical elements

PINK : sweet love, romance, softness, self love, feminine energy, innocent love

WHITE : peace, protection, divine magic, purity, blessings, cleansing and forgiveness. White can also be used to substitute any other color.

BLACK : banishing, getting rid of negative energies, dark magic, removing what no longer serves, protection of negative energy

SILVER : money (coins), intuition, attraction, physical protection

GOLD : wealth, health, success

corresponding crystals and glitters can be added to further amp up the work (see Crystals section to see which crystals go best)

QUICK CANDLE GO TO'S (6 Herbs or Less) If you don't have an Apothecary or Botanica to go to, most if not all of these herbs can be found in your local grocery store,
market, Caribbean Market, GNC, Vitamin Shoppe, Whole Foods etc.... Sometimes erroneous herbs are needed but often times they've been right under your nose the entire time.

Money Drawing
For a quick money drawing blend to attract quick cash and cash favors. Dress a green or white candle.

- Basil
- Cedar
- *Apple Pie Spice (mixture of allspice, nutmeg, cinnamon)
- Five Finger Grass
- Clove

Quick tip for Money Magic: When working with money magic remember money is an entity and energy in itself and is related to your relationship and views of money. Remember to be specific, i.e, if you need $200 but $100 is a lot to you, use your words wisely. Know that you need more than you expect; you need a major come thru, if you say you need a little money or "extra" money you may receive a $20, $40, $50 blessing, a blessing nonetheless, but only "extra money " or a "little blessing." Don't be afraid or ashamed to ask for what you want and what you need. Switching your views on money amp up what "a lot" of money means to you. Expand your desires and relationships, raise your vibration and you will receive more.

PROTECTION
A spiced up blend for spiritual protection, aura cleansing, balancing and restoring. Dress and burn a blue or white candle.

- Sage
- Bay Leaf
- Ginger
- Rosemary
- Frankincense
- Chamomile

LOVE ATTRACTION
Love drawing, mutual love attracting, platonic love and relationships, potential romantic connections. Dress a pink, red, yellow, or white candle.

- Rose
- Lovage
- Lilac
- Marigold
- Honeysuckle
- Honey

CLEAR DREAMS (MAGIC IN YOUR SLEEP)
Dress and burn before sleep to promote restful sleep and

promote lucid dreaming. Help with **Astral travel.** Dress a purple or white candle

- Lavender
- Mugwort
- Jasmine
- Star Anise

RETURN TO SENDER (JINX BREAKING/HEX REMOVING)

Used to remove any hexes, return any bad juju sent to you by someone else.

- Valerian
- Wormwood
- Black Salt
- Cayenne
- Camphor

EVIL EYE PROTECTION

To protect yourself from the evil eye or to repel or reverse effects of 'evil eye.'

- Dill
- Black Salt
- Sage
- Rue
- Verbana

4

The Cow Jumped Over the What!? (Moon Magic)

Moon Magic is by far the most powerful

Magic I have worked with. The moon gives off working vibes three days before and after, but at its peak, honey, That's where you

want to center and send out that energy! This energy can be harnessed to bring in, attract, create, banish, bind etc....

Magic can be powerful on any day, however, if you can hold off and wait for the Full Moon and the New Moon you will

experience a new and heightened sense of energy in your work. The theme of your work will correspond with whether

the Moon is Waxing(moon getting bigger; growing with light, going toward Full Moon) or Waning(moons getting smaller; decreasing in light, New Moon coming) ;

For the Waxing Moon it is best to work on items of increase, new beginnings, getting something started, refreshing and re-vitalizing, strengthening relationships and foundations. While the Waning Moon helps you to focus on themes you want to banish, bond , release , decrease or resolving conflict.

The Moon energy is a universal energy that deeply affects the world's oceans and waves, and therefore, being made up of about 65% of water ourselves, we are more often than not also affected by the moon. This is not to say that the moon will turn
you into a modern day Mystic, however, if you take the time to observe your mood and emotions you may notice a wave of
differences three days before and after the New Moon and the Full Moon. Take time to tune in around this time, drink more
water, tea, stretch, meditate and listen for any messages that the universe is sending to you to prepare for your phases. Life is cyclical and reciprocal, stay in the cycle, give more than you take but demand your worth! You'll be fine my dear.

The New Moon is the beginning of the lunar cycle and thus is appropriate for :

- new beginnings
- starting new projects
- energy revitalization time
- self care/self love
- preparation for the phase ahead
- intention setting
- enhancements
- preparing petitions for upcoming Full Moon
- herbal blending
- oil setting
- a beginning charge before fully energizing with the Full Moon power.

The energy of the New Moon is
enlightening and encouraging, go forth!

When working with the New Moon, be clear with your goals.

The New Moon is a great time to cleanse your space and invite in benevolent spirits.

Smudge and bless your space with herbs such as: Sage, Frankincense, Myrhh, Cedar, Mugwort, Lemongrass. You may want to take time to mop floors, clean altars, organize and reorganize.

Take a Spiritual Bath of some sort(coconut bath, protection bath, "Road Opener" bath, self love bath). Follow your mood.

Light white candles for gratitude, pink for self love, orange for abundance and attraction, and yellow for happiness and bright vibes.

The "7 African Powers" candle is also a great New Moon candle to refresh and touch on all areas.

FULL MOON

The Full Moon energy is probably the most potent Moon Energy you can manifest and/or banish anything under. This is simply an exhilarating and exciting energy. Anything worth waiting for can be held onto and brought to the forefront on the night of the full moon .

Full Moon magic has an unmatched Peak energy. Any manifestation that you have been holding onto up until this point is appropriate and ready to go. Unleash under the Full Moon and let your imagination and power run wild!

Big Themes include :

· Money Magic

26

- Success
- Job Drawing
- Better Business
- Love Drawing
- Strengthening Love
- Banishing unwanted themes in your life/ repetitive themes/relationships
- Sex Magic
- Charge/Cleanse Crystals
- Make Moon Water
- Let Go/Release
- Cleanse and Bless
- Divination

Full Moon magic magnifies and illuminates clarity. **ATTRACTION ATTRACTION ATTRACTION**Use the DRAW of the Full Moon.

The Full Moon is the time for your altar magic, the night of the month that values the most in manifestation. Even if you do just a small work to pay love and respect to the moon, to God or the Universal energy for the waves and vibes that she provides. A minimum of a white candle near a glass of water will do. Watch how even the small things can move greatly.

5

Express Lane: Six Items or Less

POWERFUL QUICK BLENDS (SIX INGREDIENTS OR LESS)

CUSTOMER ATTRACTION

- Frankincense or Benzoin
- Basil
- Cinnamon

Use this blend to attract more customers to your business. Burn as an incense or keep the blend in a bowl near the register. You can also burn as an incense in a place of business where you conduct financial matters.

SAGE SPRAY

- Sage
- Alcohol

- Water

For a smokeless smudge when you really need to clear the air but can't or it is not appropriate to burn sage. Any other energy clearing or restoring herbs can be added to enhance the spray.

BLACK SALT

- Salt
- Black Pepper
- ashes(metal scraping/Incense Burns)
- charcoal
- Wormwood (can be used but still effective w/o)

Black salt can be used to repel negative energy, to get rid of unwanted guest or energy, can be used in bowls to absorb negative energy, sprinkled around perimeters, thrown in the path or back path of someone leaving your home or place of business that you don't want to return.

NAWLINS FLOR D' AMOUR

- Rose
- Cinnamon
- Jasmine
- 1/4 Florida Water + 1/4 alcohol + 2/4 water

Use for attracting and emitting loving vibes. Spray in a room to enhance the mood and the vibe. To create a loving ambiance, spray on self, in your car or anywhere there needs a little love in the air.

VAN VAN (oil/floor wash/spray)

- Lemongrass
- Lemon Verbana
- Ginger
- piece of Pyrite

(add alcohol and water 50/50 for spray or floor wash)
Used to clear evil, switch bad situations to good or open the flow of new opportunities. Combine ingredients with different mediums depending on how you want to use it.

BLACK CAT INCENSE

- Myrhh
- Sage
- Bay Leaves
- Grains of Paradise (sub w/ 3/4 ginger 1/4 black pepper)

A"Witches Incense" that can be used to clear the air, keep the flow ways open, for granting wishes and keeping it going! It supports magic and success in work by cleansing, protecting, removing blockages and negativity to open the flow of the environment. Burn this when you're really in a magical mood or really in a magical slump and want energize.

MONEY RICE

- Rice (Long Grain rice as a bonus, Jasmine rice to petition luxury, etc....)
- Green Food Coloring

- Pyrite (I like to break it in pieces so it blends)
- money strips
- Magnetic Sand / gold glitter

Dye the rice with the green food coloring and let it dry completely. I like to spray a little sage spray after the color to help it dry and to bless and purify the blend. Once the food coloring dries, mix other ingredients and enjoy!

Place on an altar, in a mojo bag, near a register, or at a workstation. This rice is used to draw in and attract money to your life and especially your business.

SOUR SALT

Can be used as an additive to sour connections, to repel nuisances, to protect from irritation and emotional attacks can sprinkle on doorsteps to ward off unwanted solicitors, in front of the door of a roommate/tenant you want gone but have no real grounds to move them or in disolvingrelationships without extreme drama .

- Sea Salt
- Wormwood
- Vinegar

Add to spells to dispel, to increase sourness, thwart comfort ability, banish or get rid of without causing pain.

EASY WRATH SPRAY

Used to ease tension and animosity in a room. Spray to clear the air and encourage others to "get over" being mad with you or others. Easy Wrath Spray can also be used for keeping the energy calm when interacting with those who don't really work well with others.

- Ashes
- Black Pepper
- Cayenne
- Roses
- Alcohol
- Jasmine flowers(optional)

HOT "MOTHAFUCXIN" FOOT POWDER

Use to protect from and banish negative energy/people. Put in the tracks of enemies to bring irritation and unrest. This powder is similiar to Black Salt on beam but banishes rather than absorbs and brings a general sense of irritation and discomfort for those who track it.

- Cayenne
- Black Salt
- Sulfur
- Corn Starch
- Sour Salt
- more Cayenne

PERSUASION OIL (Do As I Say)

- Calamus
- Patchouli

- Orris Root
- Galangal
- Licorice

To get someone on your side and persuade others to see or do things your way. "Get Your Way" oil, commanding, bending, black arts.

FOUR THIEVES OIL/FLOOR WASH

Home, body and personal belonging protection. Protects home and self from thieves and swindlers. Mix with water and alcohol for floor wash, use as an addition to laundry or car washing, put in spray bottle, etc....)

- Cloves
- Lemon Zest/Lemongrass
- Cinnamon
- Eucalyptus
- Rosemary

*Can add element of spice if you like (dash of cayenne)

ROAD OPENER or ABRE CAMINO

Road opener oil used to "open the road." Open the flow for new pathways, new opportunities and opens doors in your favor.

- Orange zest/ Citron
- Lemon Verbana
- Lemongrass
- Five Finger Grass and/or Cinquefoil
- *for Latin variation replace Five Finger Grass with a sliver

of Abre Camino.

6

Artful Words: Quick Instructions on Sigils

Sigils are charged symbol spells. An intention is written and then the letters shaved down to create a symbol.

The sigil is charged in the making with intent and can be charged again by burning or letting dissolve in water. The sigil is most powerful when the intention or exact wording is forgotten except in instances with sigils such as blessing and protection i.e, bless this home, protect this house, I am protected etc....The forgetting lies more in each word written as opposed to the overall message.

It is suggested to make several at a time to more effectively "forget."

HOW TO MAKE SIGIL

Write the intention making it as plain as possible, emphasizing the message.It should be less wordy and more poetic than a written spell.

Cross out the vowels and any repeating letters.

Break letters down (a T would now look like this: _| and I can translate to _ | _ or lowercase i . |). Take the phrase "I AM" deleting "I" and "A" you are left with "M" which can be turned to |//|

A sigil is a shield of protection. It's a word generated symbol and there derives its power, the symbol created from spelling impresses itself upon the creative energy to bring about its form into the physical realm.

A lot of time, even today in the modern world that we live, symbols are more impressing or identifiable than a full name. Teams have mascots, corporations have logos. All symbols are created to spark an energy in you to associate it with its owner even if you can't specifically remember the full name. Charge up your sigils and even once you've forgotten the exact, written word the sigil becomes fully charged. The importance is conjuring and identifying the energy tied to the sigil, that is what will resonate long after the written word is forgotten.

When creating sigils take time to be intentional. The more poetic the prose or rhyming is with repeating syllables makes creating the sigil easier.

7

Black Girl Magic

Black Girl Magic is an energy, a vibe, a real genetic science. Black Girl Magic is an essence natural to Black girls and women . It is in our DNA, our Bloodline, culture and history. Its the Voodoo and Hoodoo, Santeria and Chaos Magic Arts that our ancestors conjured many moons before now. Its the natural twist of our hips, the flick of our wrist and twerk in our back.

Black Girl Magic is the Goddess within, the Queens and Warrior Women who fought and prayed and manifested before us. It is Strength and Perseverance, relentlessness and ability to impress our will and make "Something out of Nothing." We are the epitome of pressurized Diamonds.

Black Girl Magic is the revelation and realization of the energy and power of our concentrated doses of Melanin. Black Girl Magic is how our empathetic nature gives us the ample and increased power to tune into the Universal energy and Divine messages being transmitted to our World.

Conjure is and always has been a part of who we are and who we are destined to be.

Black Girl Magic is accepting, loving and walking in our

abilities. Tune into who you are. Tap into your full balance. Conquer your ego, confront your shadow and be in control of your full self. Release fear, self doubt, shame, regret, forgive yourself of any transgressions and move forward in your work. The crown has been made, it is up to you to rule and conquer yourself.

Black Girl Magic is not a trend, it is to be respected. It is fierce and very real energy. A birthright and true gift from God. Being a "Black Girl," is Magic in itself. Be loved beloved, love yourself!

8

What Time WereYou Born?

Astrology is the science of the stars, metaphorically and literally. I've read many times that the biggest group of astrology consults are millionaires. Those that know who they are, are aware of hidden character traits and are familiar with the different levels that make up who they are. When you know exactly who you are and what influences you, the more efficiently you will be able to navigate and adapt along your journey.

Many of us are already familiar with our Sun signs, the signs that are connected to our birthdays. The other two most common signs that contribute to your personality, how you view the world and how the world views you are your "moon sign," and your "rising sign." You can go online on an astrology site and generate your Natal chart which is a breakdown of your signs, and planetary influences that were apparent during your birth, or you can consult a professional Astrologer that you trust. If you're more "hands-on," do as much research as possible and figure it out for yourself. You will need name, date of birth, time of birth, and place of birth. Definitely a venture worth taking and reading to identify and highlight parts of your personality that you don't understand or have yet to confront. Included are herbal blends to coincide with each sign. These herbal blends are burned, carried, used for candle dressing or making oils to emulate the aura of each sign and to get you back in touch and line with your star self.

The Sun sign is the innermost part of you, your personality and way that you view the world. Your Moon deals with your emotional body and how you process your feeling and emotions. Your moon reflects your inner mood, how you react to the world and your Rising, which reflects the way the world sees you, your spontaneous reaction to things that happen to you or happen in the world. The Rising is the side of you that usually shows how you function in the world.

Identifying each part or yourself will help you to create a more rounded, grounded and secure version of yourself.

These blends are used to enhance and embody essence of your Sun/Moon/Rising:

AQUARIUS
   (January 20–February 18)
   Water Bearer
   Air
   *Jasmine
   *Lavender
   *Patchouli
   *Vetivert

ARIES
   (March 21–April 19)
   Ram .
   Earth

*Cinnamon
*Rose
*Galangal
*Juniper

CAPRICORN
   (December 22–January 19)
   Sea Goat
   Earth
   *Sandalwood
   *Benzoin or Frankincense
   *Patchouli

CANCER
   (June 21–July 22)
   Crab
   Water
   *Myrhh
   *Sandalwood
   *Eucalyptus
   *Lemon Peel or Oil

GEMINI
   (May 21–June 20)
   Celestial Twins
   Air
   *Gum Mastic (or other resin)
   *Citron or 1/2 lemon + 1/2 orange peel mix
   *Mace

LEO

(July 23–August 22)
Lion
Fire
*Gum Mastic (or other resin)
*Sandalwood
*Juniper Berries

SAGITTARIUS
(November 22–December 21)
Archer
Fire
*Frankincense
*Myrhh
*Clove

SCORPIO
(October 23– November 22)
Scorpion
Water
*Frankincense
*Galangal
*Pine

TAURUS
(April 20–May 20)
Bull
Earth
*Sandalwood
*Benzoin
*Rose (flower or oil)

PISCES
  (February 19–March 20)
  Two fish
  Water
  *Frankincense
  *Eucalyptus
  *Lemon Peel
  *Sandalwood (herb or oil)

VIRGO
  (August 23–September 22)
  Maiden / Goddess of Agriculture
  Earth
  *Oak moss
  *Patchouli
  *Cypress

LIBRA
  (September 23–October 22)
  Scales
  Air
  *Lavender
  *Chamomile
  *Cassia
  *Lily

43

9

When Oil and Water Mix

Oils are elixirs of herbs and a constant staple in conjure through-out time. The oils may be used to rub on hands, pulse points, hair, feet, dress candles, mojo bags, jars, intensify any incense blend, placed on money before spending, massage with intentions and whatever else you can think of. Spiritual oils are concentrated concoctions of herbs. Using your choice of oil such as Grape Seed Oil, Avocado Oil, Jojoba Oil, Olive Oil or any oil that's virtually without smell and that you are comfortable using on your skin.

Incense blends are mixed or ground in mortar and then combined in a dry glass jar. The jar can than be pressure cooked or left to soak for at least four to six weeks. I've pressured cooked my oils one time before and I still let them marinate for 6 weeks and to be honest the oils are just as concentrated if not more if you just allow the oil to absorb the essence of the herbs and soak for it's due time. I feel the scent is more fresh and equally distributed when you just let them naturally bathe in the oil for a period of time .

Oils are like the icing on the cake and supercharged! Almost any incense blend in this book can be turned into an oil. Whats more is you can use the herb guides to craft oils of your own. The main key with oils are guided measurements and patience. You must give the herbs time to fully release and the oils to fully absorb.

I always charge my oils after making them. I charge them on an altar or near a window for added moon charge with crystals and candles to energize, bless and incense the blends. Whatever you do, just be patient, natural things are better left natural.

10

Science of Magic

Magic is a Spiritual Science, it's about using Universal elements and energies, engaging the power of the mind and clearly visualizing and willing your intentions. Magic, Conjure, manifestation etc... is used to influence and manipulate energy to bend to your will, it's about attraction, clarity, faith, movement, guidance and intention.

Magical work requires a presence and being comfortable with knowing and listening. Conjure requires a desire to create and a willingness to destroy.

Conjure is about balance and following the path set in front of you.

The Law of Attraction states that there is an intangible universal energy that can be impressed upon by using your brain and visualization. Using your imagination to create and attract what you desire, then releasing the intent and energy with the faith that the Universe will create and manifest your desires is transcending. The way that everything will unfold may be unbeknownst to you and that's perfectly fine, just follow the

yellow brick road and you will find your
way.
Everything is energy!

If the world is made up and run on energy and we are energetic beings, we are all connected. We, within our DNA possess the same abilities as the Earth and the Universe, what we have in common is that we are all creators. We think it, see it, impress upon it and turn it into reality. Anything that is tangible on this earth was manifested by an energetic being.

Whatever you can dream or visualize, you can make it physically true. Visualize and see in the spiritual or "thinking realm,"extract it and process it into the physical realm. You have the power it's just up to you to activate and utilize it.

The Science of Magic is about using energy and brain matter to influence the subconscious to bring it about in reality. Science is a form of religion formulated by "Earth + Science + Faithall rolled into one. Using the laws of the Universe, the herbs, roots and crystals of the Earth and knowing of Faith (unwavering belief in the law and universal energy), you bring about your desires, designed by yourself and not by chance. Conjure is about choice, restoring, if need be and maintaining balance in your life and those around you.

It is about working with and within the flow of the Universe to attract the desires of your life. Being grateful for things that have come to pass and things that are on their way. It helps you become more expert at being the Master of your own ship.

11

Love Come Down (Sex Magic)

SEX MAGIC

Sex magic is the bomb.com and probably not used nearly as much for the amount of sex that we're having. The intensity of sex and the buildup of energy leads to orgasm which is a power energy release that can be used to heighten your intention. The Law of Attraction refers to this practice as Sexual Transmutation, using the sexual energy, especially of the orgasm to transform your reality. Sex magic can be practiced alone and also with a partner. I absolutely recommend starting this practice and starting with yourself.

Just take a second to think about the energy you harness and possess when you are sexually stimulated. It is exhilarating and often overwhelming, now imagine harnessing and controlling that power and putting it forth towards your goals and intention setting. The energy is naturally occurring and doesn't have to be forced, just navigated. The visualization can be created in your mind or you may use a physical representation of your intention to focus on at the point of orgasm. Get into the sex act as much as possible, but just remember to focus on the intention at the point of orgasm. This is also a great time to charge sigils and activate sigils with energy.

BE INTENTIONAL, SET THE MOOD

Cleanse your space, smudge the room, grab essentials if your going to be having a drink or a smoke before hand, try to keep it all in the consecrated space if possible. If you are using a physical representation make sure it is placed in a way that you can place eyes on it without having to stop and look for it. Use any oils to give yourself a massage, if using on genitals just make sure the herbs contained are safe for topical use, bring in crystals that match your intention and help set the mood. Crystals and incense are highly recommended as they contain and maintain the aura. Just be comfortable, have fun, find pleasure in finding pleasure, it will work in your favor. Self love and self care always communicate gratitude to the Universe. Set the mood if possible, but also if the mood strikes when you're laying in the middle of your laundry that you didn't feel like folding, by all means, take a hand or two, just REMEMBER, VISUALIZE AT THE POINT OF ORGASM!!

THE MAGIC OF MASTURBATION

Starting the practice on your own helps you gain control and greater understanding of the power that you are working with. It will help you to more properly harness the power, focus and remember the agenda and see it through to the end.

Leading yourself to a buildup and remembering to focus on your intention when you reach climax. When practicing Sex Magic with yourself, its just as important to set the mood and set the scene as if you were with a partner. You don't absolutely have to, but it adds to the ambiance, keeps you focused and helps you stay in the magic mood.

Masturbation makes sure you take time for yourself, curbs anxiety, deepens self understanding and self love and increases spiritual connection when done with intention. Masturbation is favorable when manifesting, it's such a commanding and strong standpoint taking your pleasure in your own hands. It's very naturally akin to taking your life into your own hands and becoming the Creator of your own destiny rather than waiting for someone to bring pleasure into or change to your life. Take some time and get close with yourself.

When doing Sex Magic with a partner its best that both partners know the vibe so the energy isn't thwarted and focus can be properly maintained. Its simple as telling your partner you want to manifest something with the energy created when having sex with each other. It can be a fun experiment, you both can decide and think of something you really want to manifest. Setting the mood helps you stay focused because when using a partner its best to peak and reach orgasm at the same time. You can start with something small to get comfortable or go in "gong ho," it's purely up to you, it's just best that it's something that both parties are comfortable with.

*Controlling your breathing helps as it assist you in harnessing the energy and buildup to a Worthy Orgasm and that's a tip for sex and magic.

Themes to look into to increase power in Sex Magic :

· Kudalini
· Breathing Exercises
· Sexual Transmutation

COMMON HERBS FOR SEX MAGIC :

- Hibiscus
- Blue Lotus
- Catnip
- Ginseng
- Mint
- Orange
- Patchouli
- Violet
- Periwinkle

12

More than Rocks (Crystal Section)

Crystals are gifts from the Earth and full of popping JuJu! I carry crystals everywhere, in my bag, in my car, in my purse, my pockets,

I wear them, place them in my plants, my altars,my mojo bags and crystals. Stones have a pure grounding energy and are literally the art of the Earth at your fingertips.

The energy is apparent in just being around crystals. Touching them is another story and using them in your everyday life for spells and rituals is Magic.

BEGINNER CRYSTALS

ROSE QUARTZ : Love
   CITRINE : Happiness, abundant success
   CLEAR QUARTZ : meditation, clarity, focus
   TIGERS EYE : success, strength, endurance, luck with business
   TOURMALINE : protection, banishing negative energy
   JADE : oney, opportunity, protects against ill health and

poverty

AGATE : grounding , stability,

LAPIS LAZULI : protective, wisdom and truth , enhances intellectual abilities , communication and harmony, awareness

AMETHYST : Healing, protective energy , calming, prevents psychic attack ,emotional and physical attack , protects against environmental attacks

Amethyst ranges from a light translucent purple to a deep translucent purple. A quick go to for a true calming stone and

promoter of tranquil sleep. Carry Amethyst during stressful situations and when you generally want to keep calm.

A "relax and carry on" stone

Rose Quartz whether raw or tumbled is a sweet pink hue. Perfect crystal when you want to radiate and/or attract love.

Rose quartz brings an all around feeling of love and light. Sweet feelings, romantic feelings, unconditional love.

Sweeten your aura, feelings, mood, mend a broken or bruised heart. A definite "Love" stone.

Citrine ranges from a light translucent yellow, deep yellow orange to a deep brownish orange with a hint of brightness.

Citrine is a definite stone to elicit happiness and happy feelings to attracting abundance into your life.

A happy abundant stone, the look of Citrine screams "happy abundance" a definite "feel good" stone. Attracting good

vibes to promote that and put you in the flow of attraction.

Tiger's Eye is always a brown stone with gleams of a goldenyellow. A beautiful go to and one of my favorites. Tiger's

Eye promotes confidence, strength, success in business dealings is an energy booster and supporting crystal. Take with you

when dealing with business matters, jobs, interviews, promotions, important speaking commitments, big events. Use when

you need that confidence booster to land the "punches" A "get-ish done" stone.

Clear Quartz is almost like a white candle but better! Its really a wonder to stare thru a piece of Earth and still feel

it's amazing powerful benefits. Clear Quartz is a clearing, clarifying, clairvoyance boosting stone. "The Healing Stone," Clear Quartz clarifies everything, helps you to connect closer to the spiritual realm and allows you to manifest with a boost of energy not found in any other. The Clear Quartz "heals connections," it reconnects us to spirits when we are out

of wack to help regenerate and get us back to our whole forms. Meditate with this stone and watch your life change.

TOURMANLINE is a deep black crystal heavy on the protection and the negative energy repellent. The Tourmaline actually

absorbs the negative energy and transform it to a lighter tone. Its a "Situation Flipper" stone. Keeps you grounded and

balanced by keeping a protective aura around you that negative energies just literally cannot penetrate. Great stone

to keep with you at all times or in a general vicinity. Don't be afraid of the Black, this beauty plays well with others.

13

Not a Change Bag: A Note on Mojo Bags

MOJO BAGS

The tried and true way of carrying your JuJu with you is "Mojo Bags." Mojo bags are little drawstring bags, usually flannel for durability but any material is fine. I've used silk but, I recommend silk for bags that aren't handled as much. Silk bags can be used for home mojo bags that will be hung, or placed in a car or any intention that you want to be "smooth as silk" for.

Mojo bags are derived traditionally from the Hoodoo culture, carrying and placing out of sight herbs and talisman that you want to carry for whatever reason. Its about carrying this bag and infusing it with energy like you carry your wallet or purse. Unlike the jars, items can be added, refreshed, switched out, etc... to change or increase intention. You can continuously carry, tend to, energize and feed your intention with the Mojo bags. Mojo bags are goodie bags full of herbs, crystals, talismans, oils, salts and full of intention to carry on ones person, home or in vehicle for protection or carried attraction. Mojo bags increase with energy as you use, place and carry them.

I love a good Mojo Bag, the material allows the essence to easily flow and it's easily carried and put away.

WHAT YOU NEED

- drawstring Bag
- crystal(s) corresponding to need (Tourmaline for protection, Jade for money, Rose for love and, Pyrite for attraction)
- Herbs/Oils (Sage for protection, Come To Me Oil for attraction, Basil for money, Galangal for court)
- Curios, Talisman (evil eye blocker, small picture, statue)
- Bay Leaf (write an intention)
- Pair of Lodestone (optional but heavy on the attraction)

MOJO BAG EXAMPLES:

FAVORS

- Five finger grass
- Cinnamon
- Allspice
- Aventurine
- Honeysuckle

GOT YOU COVERED (HOME PROTECTION BAG)

- Basil
- Hyssop
- Rue

- Bay Leaf
- Star Anise
- Black Salt
- Dill
- Evil eye talisman, bead, image or protection sigil
- Lapis Lazuli and/or Black Tourmaline

SLEEP SATCHET

- Jasmine
- Amethyst
- Lavender
- Mugwort

NO SHADE (EVIL EYE BLOCKER)

- Sage
- Lime Rind
- Black Salt
- Rue
- Onyx
- Dill
- Evil Eye Blocker Bead

FIRM FEET (STAY GROUNDED/CENTERED)

- Calendula
- Lemon Balm

- Valerian
- Tigers Eye

Money Bag

- Jade and/or Pyrite
- Bay Leaf (with intention)
- High John Root
- pair of Lodestone
- actual money
- some type of money oil, come to me oil, attraction oil

14

Clair-What??

Divination is using physical means to tap into the divine and communicate with the spiritual world about what is, what was or what is to come in the physical. Divination is used to gain spiritual insight or foretelling information, it's like a "phone line" to the spirits. There are many different types of Divination and ways to connect, knowing which ways provide you more clarity and will help you to better discern and interpret the messages you receive.

Identifying your method of discernment is important because it will help you to fine tune your spiritual antenna by focusing on your strengths and will also help you to figure out your "go-to" when doing purposeful divination. You may be one that receives messages at random all the time however, Divination is the intentional ritual to receive downloads. Divination is about looking into the future, marginalizing the present and delving into the path.

Even if you know nothing about any of these subjects, I am positive that you are familiar with at least a few methods of divination. The gift is in you, the communication lines are open and we are all born with an automatic download of the phone book, we literally only have to "dial(tune) in."

A few common methods include Tarot, meditation, scrying, free writing, dance, song, art or cooking, truly, whatever moves your soul and activates those endorphins and Pineal Gland (Third Eye).

TAROT

The infamous tarot is one of the oldest card tricks in the book and the gag is, there is no trick, the cards don't lie. That is not to say that the interpretation is always spot on, but from all of my experience with the Tarot, it still hasn't ceased to surprise me with how spot on it is.

Tarot is the method where one uses cards, a traditional playing card deck but more often than not, some form of the traditional Tarot deck. The reader then uses the cards to usually ask a question or make aware the desire to receive whatever message the spirit has for them. Often people come to ask specific questions, get help facing the present, hear optional paths for the future and make aware influential people and themes already in their life that are either coming or going.

Each card belongs to a set or suit and have a number of character images attached. Each suit deals with different themes and the numbers and character images represent "sub-themes." The original and today's deck offers another set of twenty-two cards that are called the "Major Arcana." These cards represent a major force in your life, a change, a "strong hold," or new beginnings. Major Arcana represents "major deals."

**A few cards in the Major Arcana include cards such as "The Fool," for blissful beginnings, a "new-comer,"the blissful igno-

rance of being a Freshman daring and carefree, "The Fool" en-courages one to go forth with changes and new beginnings with an excited, encouraged attitude. Relish in your transition! "The Empress," who represents femininity, beauty, abundance, success in the marketplace, the birth of new ideas, pleasure and being and getting in touch with your feminine side (money is a feminine energy, get familiar) and the long feared "Death" card. The Death Card is actually an overall great card when it comes to change, ultimately representing the ending and discarding of old or "dead" themes, situations, and relationships in your life and starting something new. The Death card is more related to endings that include natural beginnings, birth/rebirth, transition and transformation. Death is not to be feared but respected as is the entire deck. Anyone can read tarot or you can seek out the reading of a trusted reader or you can do this divination method (like all others) on your own. The key with the tarot is to have a general understanding or willingness to research and tune in for supporting themes.

AUTOMATIC WRITING

You've probably done this one a million times. Automatic writing is letting your brain clear with a pen and paper and writing about nothing in particular, letting the spirit guide your hand. In the beginning, it's random themes, pop up thoughts, side notes, etc.... Once you continue and stick with it , it begins to flow. You have to allow yourself to write freely, to not think too much or hesitate, but just write what you are receiving. Many times this is where you find grand ideas as well as glimpses into the future. Writing is spelling and spelling is divination in itself. I have many times went back into old notebooks and found things that were "profound" for me.

SCRYING

Scrying is the method in foretelling that works with a reflec-tive object such as a crystal ball or a mirror, smoke and water. The practice includes dazing into these mediums until images and messages begin to emerge. This method can also be used to stare into fire or flame, it's reflective properties have also been known to reveal many messages and images as it's a natural divination method in magic. It's sort of a meditation with your eyes open!

More relaxed forms of divination are art, dance, song or painting .Dance and song have long been used in ritual, church and magical culture and is still relevant today. Turning up the right mood boosting and energy centering music and dancing and singing when completely letting go can be transcending. The key is to allow yourself to go into a lifted state to be in a place to receive divine massages and signs. Getting to a place that lifts you above all of your apparent worries, elevates vibrations and therefore, elevates your attraction game and clears any blocked pathways to get information to you. Just purposely move, go into these movements and actions with questions and focused themes, let go and see what comes back to you.

How do you receive and process messages and information from the spiritual realm?

We all learn and process differently, therefore it makes sense that we interpret spiritual messages and divination differently as well. There are many different ways to process, a few general themes to describe these methods are:

Clairvoyance which means "clear vision." Someone who is clairvoyant sees their message as a clear picture, much like the psychic scenes in the Disney show "That's So Raven," it's all about the Second or Third Eye Vision premonition.

Clairvoyance gives you an audience view into the scenes of what have happened or things to come.

Clair-audient beings are those that hear the spirit or the message as someone is in the room with them. They receive verbal messages that they then discern and often don't have to as the spirits may send the message as clear as day.

Clair-sentient are those that feel the feels. The ones that just know because they feel it in their bones and spirit. These beings are also great with feeling where the spirit is, differentiating and discerning positive and negative entities and reading other's auras and energies. They have the ability to really read a place.

Clair-tangency is knowing through touch, by receiving messages, images, feelings and touching items or people.

Often depicted as seers and diviners who help police locate people through touching their belongings or something that holds the energy of the event that took place.

15

Protect Yuh Neck (Protection Magic)

Protect your neck!

I can not express this enough!! "Pruh-teck Yuh Neck!"

Protection magic is of the utmost importance. It is another form of self care. Making sure you are protected whether you are dealing with dark energy or light. Protection magic is like strapping in your seat belt, looking both ways before you cross the street, placing an alarm in your home. Exercising preventative measures for health and safety on the spiritual realm is as important as it is on the physical realm.

A lot of practitioners or people who are drawn to the craft tend to be Empaths. An Empath is someone who is sensitive to the feelings, energy and hidden emotions of others. They tend to absorb the energy and receive its effects, this can be a spiritual drain. A protective measure for Empaths would be to carry protective stones such as Black Tourmaline, for a spiritual force field taking negative energies and turning them around, Amethyst, for calm protective peace, or Smokey Quartz, which transmutes negative energy to positive. Smokey Quartz is similar to Black Tourmaline, but also detoxifies your body and it's environment.

SMUDGING

Smudging is the burning of herbs, roots, resins, incense to allow the essence of the smoke to fill and clear out and/or restore the energy of the room or environment. It is important to **open your windows when smudging** as it allow the negative energy to escape and allows the smoke to leave and clear the air. Sage and Palo Santo are two very popular smudging methods. Sage is used to clear the air and room of negative energy, it promotes cleansing and healing properties. You can also sage yourself and others, waving the wand in a symbolic cleansing away from the top of your head to the bottom of your feet. Smudge your third eye and the rest of your chakras (smudge yourself in a vertical motion over the front of your body). Sage is often sold in a smudge stick form and is a light grey velvety leaf. A thick distinct odor that may be an acquired taste, but is definitely an herb worth acquiring. Sage does a complete sweep. We joke in the conjure community that if you enjoy the sage, that's great, and if you don't then that's good to because that means its doing its job! Use sage to remove the negative energies, work with this herb for a while and you will revel in it's effect.

Palo Santo is also a very common method of smudging and is also used for cleansing and purifying the energy of the room, person and mood. Palo has an uplifting quality as it restores the energy and has a more sweet aroma than Sage. It's a wooden burn and doesn't hold a fire as long as Sage but also a less amount of smoke is needed to do it's job. Burn before rituals, after sage or anytime you just want a quick mood lifter. Light wood sticks usually cut into six inch rectangular cubes.

Other agents that are common for smudging include but are not limited to:

- Lemongrass
- Frankincense
- Cedar
- Mugwort
- Lavender
- Myrhh
- Sweetgrass

Smudging can be done daily or when you feel the energy or if the air is "getting thick," things start going "out of wack," you're feeling spiritually "heavy" or drained, or simply after you clean a space or your house.

Smudging is different from burning incense in that it's specifically geared to cleansing, purifying, and restoring energies and getting rid of negative energy or all residual energy in the room. Other herbs may be added to smudge sticks and burns to play supporting roles. Materials can also be burned on a charcoal disk.

Sage burns really well and really holds the burn, take caution when burning Sage as it has a tendency to burn to the end if not snuffed out.

Charcoal burns work best in ceramic or cast iron pots and can also be placed upon a bed of salt or sand to conduct the heat. Some material can only be burned on charcoal such as resins like Frankincense and Myrrh, which are great protective and clarifying blend. I recommend burning in a ceramic bowl or pot, placing the herbs first and placing the charcoal on top of the herbs as the herbs seem to burn faster and denser when burned on top. Open the Windows and smudge on!

Other common protective go-to herbs include :

- Basil
- Chamomile
- Rosemary
- Rue
- Hyssop
- St. Johns Worth
- Camphor
- Valerian Root
- Galangal Root
- Dill
- Juniper
- High John the Conqueror
- Thyme

16

Spiritual Allies

If you don't know where to start in the spiritual world as far as communicating and who to communicate with, the first reach out I recommend is to your ancestors and passed on loved ones. If we have any allies in the spiritual realm, it is more than likely going to be the people who were apart of your bloodline and DNA. You are most familiar with these energies and should be able to easily discern and properly provide suitable offerings. Not only that, they are probably waiting for you to reach out and are probably especially eager if you have made petitions and offerings to other entities and spirits. Continue your relationships into the spiritual realm because that energy is divinely yours to interact with.

After they pass, spirits tend to continue to like certain things that they favored when they were on the physical realm. For instance, if your grandmother liked butterscotch candy when she was here, its a nice little treat to leave butterscotch on the altar. Maybe you had an uncle that was good with getting quick cash and liked cognac. Leave him some cognac and petition him for his help or just leave him some cognac just to say "hey, thinking about you." Your family will show up for you.

You can create an altar for your loved ones that passed, to honor them, for guidance, protection, assistance, etc.... An ancestor altar can be as elaborate or simple as you like but usually include at least the following :

- A picture of Ancestors (spiritual element)
- A Candle (Fire)
- A glass of Water
- Incense (Air)
- Crystal (Earth)
- Any talisman or object of representation of family or individual members

It is also customary to "feed the ancestors," making them plates when the family eats dinner, special meals, birthday meals, celebration meals, gratitude meals. Place the food on the altar until the "essence" is gone and then discard as you choose. . Feed your ancestors, you will see random blessings show up in you life and you will feel more open and connected to your passed relatives.

You don't have to over feed your ancestors, keeping a glass of water is key. You can create a ritual or routine like "Coffee on Mondays, Teas on Tuesday, Friday Night Wine and Dinner," whatever you choose just let it be a notion to let them know that you are thinking of them.

ANCESTOR MONEY

You can leave for your ancestors or burn real money as an offering, to pay generational debts and to petition for more cash flow to you. You can also buy pre-printed "Ancestor Money" to offer and burn. Placing real cash is nice and energetic, but I recommend also buying "Ancestor Money" as it is specific to them and you get more "burn for your buck."

Pay homage to your bloodline, do work in breaking generational curses and creating new traditions and you will see your work increase, manifestation return time improve and overall improvement of quality of life. Be consistent.

17

Watah

Water is the Universal element that connects every living, breathing being on this planet. This is what we have in common, our make up, our need for water, our draw, our reverence for water's effects and its life giving ways and ability to destroy.

Water is our Medium.

Water is the sustaining, ever creating, moving life force that connects us on the physical world to the spiritual world.

When doing any work it always a good idea to have water near, it is always a necessary offering when working with saints, ancestors and usually spirits in general. Water is not only an offering, it's also a means of communication.

Water in Conjure is about Duality.

Literally like offering a guest a glass of water or inviting someone in for a glass of water but also knowing that "inviting someone in for a glass of water" is "code" for an invitation to communicate.

"I am offering you this glass of water in case you are thirsty and to let you know that I am aware of the "code" if you wanted to communicate."

For a long time water has been a portal opener and bridge between the spirit and physical realm. Place out a glass of water and watch a blessing flow.

Also, on a major health note that pertains to clarity, drinking water will clear physical and spiritual blockages making you more susceptible to the spirit and messages from the Universe. Drink water when doing work to avoid stagnation and to have on hand in case "ish" goes down! Drinking water and keeping clean water around will keep you balanced and in a nice flow.

Even the water of the Earth is related to religion and conjure since the beginning of time. Using the ponds, rivers and oceans to guide or to baptize, it only makes sense that today we still heavily affiliate water with magic and incorporate it into our work.

OTHER FORMS OF WATER AND THEIR USES:

RAIN WATER / STORM WATER : Water collected during a rainstorm and stored . Storms are always a great time to collect water, whether the storm be calm or crazy. I love using calm rainstorm water for blessings, purification, floor washes, home sprays, personal foot soaks and for powerfully calming and relaxing effects. I also use the calm rain water to water my plants.

THUNDERSTORM WATER for heavy protection, deep cleansing, war water. Lightning storms are especially good for war water. Storm water is super charged simply from the energy and electricity that comes along with the storm.

FLORIDA WATER: to cleanse, purify, renew and refresh your

aura and the aura in the room. Long famous for its refreshing qualities, Florida water refreshes the soul, a spiritual cleanser that leaves a positive balance. Use to cleanse and anoint your hands, magical objects, living and ritual space, cleanse attached energies and calm high energy and high traffic places.

- Lemon Verbana
- Cinnamon
- Bergamot
- Basil
- Hyssop
- Cloves
- Cedar
- Rose
- Mint
- Lemon Balm
- Lavender Alcohol Witch Hazel (for moisture)

Florida water can be played with in different variations just keep in mind it's a crisp clean smell and usually always contains light floral notes, a clean zest, a subtle mint and supporting green cleansing and protective herbs.

HOLY WATER : Retrieved from a church or blessed on your own with a little salt and praying Psalm 23 while holding the water until you are satisfied.

ROSE WATER : Tea Boil Roses and add Vitamin E oil can be added to help preserve. This oil can be used on the skin, hair, nails and when creating love spells. This water should be refrigerated if Vitamin E oil is not added.

WAR WATER: Used to end war or strife between someone and/or wreak havoc on them. In the old days one would break a jar of war water on the target's front porch. If this is not possible to do, throw the water on the person's lawn or use in a spell with their picture. You can also place their picture in a jar of water and break it at a different location while visualizing that you are breaking it on their porch. War water can also be sprinkled around your perimeter for protection and to remove disruptive forces.

*Spanish Moss (use wormwood and/or cayenne as substitute for Spanish Moss)

*Pond Water/Swamp Water/ Storm Water

18

Bath-Time! Let's Talk About Spiritual Baths

If you've never had a spiritual bath, take one this week.

Spiritual baths are about cleansing and enhancing the spirit by soaking and/or rinsing in the essence of blessed herbs. Deeply connected to self care, self love and taking the time out for yourself. I literally feel high after a spiritual bath. I feel lifted, rejuvenated and divine after a spiritual bath.

Spiritual Baths are a great way to recharge and rejuvenate your energy and life flow. Spiritual baths have been traditionally associated with religions such as Santeria , Hoodoo and Voodoo. Other practices incorporate the bath but with less restrictions.

I'm here to tell you that you can take a spiritual bath whether you practice a religion or not. A spiritual bath is a bath charged with herbs, essential oil, flowers, etc.... The bath can be a full bath where the herbs and oils are laid directly into the bath or placed in a tea bag, allowing the essence to escape into the water.

If you don't have a bath or don't want or like to bathe, you can take a "head bath." A head bath can be had in the shower by placing the herbs or tea bag in a water bowl and pouring the water over your head. You will brew the bath in a pot or let it soak in a bowl or bucket of hot water until it cools. The herbs and oils should coincide with the flows that you would like to open, i.e, money bath, sweet bath, spiritual cleansing bath, protection bath, good vibes, self love, channeling feminine/masculine energy.

There is a bath and herb for EVERYTHING! My personal favorite is a loose herb and flower, full hot bath with Epsom salt and coconut oil. I like to feel and rub the herbs on my skin while soaking and visualizing my intentions.

This ritual is akin to Baptisms, being dunked into the Holy Water and coming out of the water anew.

It is recommended to take a shower scrub or already be physically clean before the bath. In the religious or cultural tradition, it is customary to be clean because one is not encouraged to wash off after the bath as to not interfere with the essence of the herbs. Work is supposed to be minimal after the bath and is often encouraged to take before bed. It is also customary to dress in all white head to toe after the bath and sleep in white. It's completely up to you, I personally do a quick rinse or use a corresponding soap and/or scrub to wash before or after, it really just depends on how I feel. The essence is absorbed but if you have hygienic trends that nudge you to wash after, by all means take a shower. Dry, moisturize, and reap the blessings!!

When I am taking a soaking bath, I always set the mood and scene as with any ritual. Make sure to first clean your space, bath, bathroom, I like to splash the tub with Florida water after cleaning it then smudge the air with herb or incense of your choice. The mood can be enhanced with candles, crystals and incense to match intentions.

There are as many variations of baths as there are teas, you can create your own blend and try the few I provide.

DIVINE TIMING BATH

- Coconut Milk : luxe, deep moisture, invite good spirits, spiritual cleansing and protection.
- Rue : ward off evil eye, purifying, attract positive people
- Jasmine : abundance, attractiveness
- Lime : protection, abundance , attraction
- Epsom Salt : soaking, protective
- Vetivert : prosperity, protection, grounding assisting

LIFT ME UP, KEEP ME GROUNDED : For lifting your mood and aura, clearing pathways and opening opportunities while keeping you "grounded" and aware of what's going on around you. Best to take at night to wake up feeling anew.

- Bergamot : protection and prosperity, improves memory promotes restful sleep
- Orange : increase attractiveness and abundance
- Basil : protective, cleansing, luck drawings, protects against mental attack
- Kava Kava Root Success, muscle relaxant, calming
- Sandalwood : manifestation, concentration, flow opening, chakra healing
- Patchouli : charm and attraction
- Calendula : attract admiration, networks, friendship; happiness

SWEET BATH:

· Lemon Verbana

*Add any other citrus tones, sweetening herbs you like or just rock with the Verbana. It's a bath to sweeten your aura and attraction.

COMMON HERBS FOR SPIRITUAL BAT

· Rue
· Hyssop
· Eucalyptus
· Verbana
· Marjoram
· Frankincense Oil
· Lemon/Lime
· salt
· Basil
· Holy Water
· Lavender
· Chamomile
· Bay leaves
· Roses

*If you can drink it in a tea, you can make it into a bath, get creative with the blends and see what you can manifest and release with a Spiritual Bath.

19

Affirmations

- I am strong.
- I am blessed.
- I am capable.
- I am capable of taking care of myself.
- I am a provider.
- I am worthy.
- I am more than my work.
- I am open to new opportunities.
- I am open to growth.
- I am grateful.
- I am grateful for having things to be grateful for.
- I am open to love.
- I am open to giving and receiving blessings.
- I am blessed.
- I am a blessing.
- I am a money magnet.
- I am confident.
- I am ready for new opportunities when they arrive.

- I am loved
- I am learning new things everyday.
- I am committed to bettering myself with each opportunities that arise.
- I am in control of my emotions and actions.
- I am the master of my ship.
- I am aligned .

20

Rituals, Spells & Making Your Own

Some conjure requires no words in that the written petition or the mere mixture of herbs, roots, crystals and elements are communication enough to the Universe.

While others feel the work is not complete until actions have been performed and words spoken. A common one word expression used often in conjure is "Ase'." It is literally inserting, directing or infusing your intention with life energy. It is akin to "It is so," "Amen," and "So mote it be."

Working spells and rituals is combining everything you know and incorporating the elements of magic, action, attraction and gratitude to imprint your intention on the Universe. It's like religious ceremonies, such as, "eating the flesh, drinking the blood and prayer," praying over food before eating it, ritual habits, making smoothies and twenty minutes of exercise daily to improve your health. It's about performing actions and rituals to effect change in the present and the future. There is a plethora of rituals and spells that you could perform, there are so many in this world you could practice a new one everyday. However rituals consume a lot of energy so pick and choose wisely which things and people are worth the energy required when performing rituals and doing magic in general. You can perform tried and true spells and rituals or you can start a book and create you own, it's completely up you. Here are a few rituals that have worked for me in my work :

PROTECTION RITUAL (home, body and/or spirit)

For protection of home and body, purifying, jinx removing, negative energy, banishing, promoting and restoring positive energy.

Take the time to physically clean your entire house, especially main areas like the kitchen, dining room ,living room, bathrooms, doorways, etc.... Cleaning your room is also a good idea as this is where you sleep. After you clean your house, wind down and take a spiritual bath for cleansing and protection. After your bath, even if you have already smudged the place, smudge the entire place and yourself once more. Some of the herbs from the bath can also be included in the smudging if you choose to let the aura and aroma continue for a while. Use a white or blue candle or both, write your name three to nine times on the candle imagining a protective light force and collective as you write and petition for protection. Bless the candle with your choice of protection oil, if you don't have any specific protection oil, Olive Oil is fine. Continue to focus and visualize as you rub the candle or dress the candle with oil. Ritual Candles are preferred candles in this ritual, a glass set "7-day" candle can be used to burn in the background to continue energy after spell candles burn out. Now, the candle can be dressed with Hyssop or left alone. Place a small pile of salt around the bottom of the candle, set out a glass of water and repeat:

"Bless this body, this home, this spirit
   Dispel any negativity that dare venture near it
   Protection of the highest power, may evil fear it
   That I keep going forward and never grow weary"

Repeat three to nine time or until satisfied.

While the candles burn, construct a few "Got You Covered" protection bags (see *Mojo Bags)* for your home, self and family members. Sage the bags and hang them in a window, in the front or back of home or above front or back door. The Mojo bag can also be carried on your person or in your car.
   An herbal tea is recommended to help you wind down and center yourself.
   This mixture can be used for your bath and can also be used to mop floors :
SPIRITUAL PROTECTION BLEND

- Rue
- Rosemary
- Hyssop
- Pinch of Dill
- Lime
- Eucalyptus
- Bay Leaf
- Carnation

FAST LUCK/ QUICK MONEY SPELL
   This ritual includes creating a bowl that will be charged to attract quick money and luck in gambling. After the bowl is created you can transfer the blend to a small vial that can be

carried and continuously charged thereafter when you need it. The ritual consist of making the jar and charging it. A "Fast Luck Oil" recipe is listed below to increase the potency of the spell. The oil needs to be made at least 4-6 weeks in advance or you may purchase it from a trusted source.

Items you will need include:

- a glass bowl
- Cinnamon or pieces of Cinnamon stick
- piece of Vanilla bean
- pair of Lodestone
- piece of Pyrite
- Magnetic Sand
- a lot of Sugar
- Patchouli
- gold coin
- Fast Luck Oil

As always, smudge your environment. You can drink an herbal blend to get you in the mood, such as, "Luxury on Ice" *(Witch's Brewery) as you are mixing and getting your items*ingredients together.

Line the bottom of your bowl with Patchouli,place the Pyrite,the gold coin, the cinnamon stick of powder and vanilla bean on top of the herb. Fully cover the top with the "Fast Luck Oil. " Now, fully cover the mixture with sugar. Take the Lodestone pair and place them on top of the sugar bed and then feed the Lodestone pair with Magnetic Sand. Light four candles around the bowl in a "crossroad" fashion, a variation of red, green, gold and orange candles. Light the candles and repeat this mantra three to nine time or until you are satisfied.

"Money, money come to me fast,
Flip it and tip it in multiple bags,
Money, Money come to me fast
Much let it be and long let it last"

Feed the lodestone a little more magnetic sand to top it off. Now, daily for 3 days after, light a white spell candle and feed a little magnetic sand to your lodestone pair. Keep a clean glass of water near your bowl. At end of three days, contents of the bowl can be placed in a jar or vial, charged with a white candle and used from there on.

CANT HOLD ME (BEAT THE CASE COURT SPELL)

To sway the judge and/or jury in your favor, to receive a lighter judgement. Items include:

- Galangal Root
- Lo John
- Cloves
- Cedar

When executing this ritual it is important that you use your hand and intention. To further incense and energize your intention, I recommend grinding the Galangal and Lo John by hand as opposed to buying the powder. Galangal is also a powerful court root on its own and I recommend to carry in your pocket for favor when dealing with less severe cases). Take the ground herbs and mix in a mortar with the Cloves and Cedar.

Burn this mixture on charcoal for fourteen days leading up to your court case or trial. When lighting incense, use the incantation:

"May I be smooth like silk
   May my enemies spoil like milk
   No more than a pinch may I walk away clean
   That it end abruptly in your favor, a sweet, sweet dream."

Save and collect the ashes, place them in a green or brown silk Mojo bag along with this written incantation and place in your pocket or carry bag when showing up for court.

RETURN TO SENDER (Hex Breaking and Jinx Removing Ritual). This ritual is used when you feel like someone has done work against you, is sending you the evil eye or has cast a hex or jinx in your name. This blend and ritual works in a way to not only remove the jinx but to take the energy and return it to the one who sent it to you. The blend is designed to protect, cleanse and find its way back to it's creator!

This ritual consists of dressing a candle and a bath and letting the herbs do their job. I recommend taking a "Return to Sender" bath first with the herbal blend. You will cleanse yourself and then cleanse your space, it is best that you have your incense blend already prepared and everything ready to go.

Now, visualize the person that sent bad juju your way, if you dont know who it is just imagine the JuJu being removed and pulled into a ball away from you and shooting off back to the original source. Dress your candles, if you have a name, write that name three to nine times on paper and place face down on a mirror, place the candle on top of the name if you have one or directly on top of the mirror. Light the candle and repeat:

"May what's been sent to me be returned
   With this candle light may you feel the burn

I clear my head and remove my jinx
With God and the Universe may I be in sync.

Repeat this mantra three to nine times or until you are satisfied.

Once the candle burns out, put the pictures, ashes, leftover wax and a little black salt and the mirror in a bag, dispose of the items at a crossroad, landfill, large dumpster or graveyard, whichever is closer or resonates closest with you. Throw or place to the left, walk away and don't look back!

BETTER BUSINESS RITUAL : to increase business, sales, profit , customer drawing, ideas and overall business boost. This is a simple ritual that can be done when business is slow or business is consistent but you're ready to handle more. Items needed :

- Glass Bowl
- Money Rice (*Quick Blends*)
- Pyrite, Tigers Eye or Citrine
- Frankincense
- Basil
- Magnetic Sand
- Lodestone
- Sweet Orange Essential Oil
- Cinnamon)

Best if done in place of business but can also be done where you handle your business, money, business altar or idea space. Fill a glass bowl with money rice, if money rice doesn't include Pyrite already then place a stone in money rice along with your Lodestone pair. Place an image of your logo, business card, or picture of your business on an altar under the rice bowl. Light four spell candles or one "7 day candle," "Better Business," or "Road Opener," candle. If using spell candles, light a variation of orange, yellow and green candles. Dress the candle with Sweet Orange oil. Burn Basil, Frankincense and Cinnamon as incense on charcoal tablets. Burn the candle and repeat:

May my mind be at peace as my business increase
   God bless the chief
   When I am awake and when I am asleep
   Carts on heap, customers on repeat
   May I move with courage and be met with success
   May my stock go up and my books be blessed

Keep a clean glass of water near your money rice bowl and feed your lodestone and rice bowl with magnetic sand daily.

EYES LIKE MIRRORS

"Eyes like Mirrors" Truth Revelation Spell is used when you need to see or would like someone else to see the clear intentions and character of the people around. Take a look from behind the mirror and see what truths will be revealed!

Make sure you want to see what you want to see or make sure you're kosher so the one that you want to see, sees you in a good light.

Items needed for this ritual include:

Eyebright

Vetivert

Rose

Orris Root

Blue, black and silver candle (2) white candles

small mirror

Quartz Crystal

Black Salt/Camphor Blend

Dress blue, black and silver candle together with incense blend. I like to bind candles to burn together.

Place a picture of yourself or someone else facing up (eyes toward back of mirror). Dress the candle with "Obatala Oil" or Olive Oil. Place candle triad on top of mirror and sprinkle black salt and camphor mixture around the perimeter of mirror. Recite the following:

"Truth concealed

let truth be revealed

As the candle burns let true colors prevail

May you(I) see them for who they are

Plain as day and bright as stars

True colors hidden

May your facade be ridden!!

Repeat three times or as many times as you feel necessary.

Light triad of candles and let burn out, once triad burns out, light and burn a white candle dressed and placed where the triad burned out. Discard as you choose.

MAKING YOUR OWN

Making your own spells is not only fun but charged up with your specific intention and will. Set the intentions, pick the right items, decide if you will use incantations. If you will then create one. Rhyming creates a flow and helps keep it as simple as possible to help you remember, keep it smooth and to help let the words roll off your tongue seamlessly into the Universe. Use as many of the Universal elements that you can incorporate

(Fire, Air, Earth, Water). Trust yourself and trust your magic!

*Tip: when performing rituals and impressing intent it's often helpful to incorporate music that puts you in the mood of your intention.

21

Herbes de JuJu(Herbs & Their Magical Properties

BEGINNER HERBS (A-Z)

A

Allspice : Attracting money and luck / increases energy in spell.

Alkanet Root : Prosperity, burned to purify negativity; Attract Prosperity, Increase wealth and luck in business & gambling

B

Bay Leaf : Health, Success, Enhance spiritual gifts, increase wisdom/clarity/insight (write intentions/wishes or things you wish to banish then burn)

*Take some Bay leaves, sage the space the leaves, and write your intentions and wishes on the Bay Leaf, burn the leaves and let your wishes and intention go into the air. Take a set of leaves and write all of the things you want to change or banish and burn those leaves.

Basil : Business attraction, wealth, customer draw, Protection, attract money, success, prosperity

C

Catnip : Used to enhance happiness, women's love herb, Makes men follow women like children , beauty , makes women enticing, attracts friendship *Hold in hand until warm then hold anyone's hand and they will be your friend forever.

Calendula : Love and constancy, spiritual powers, happiness, sunny disposition traditional "he loves me he loves me not" flower.

Chamomile : Good luck , luck in gambling , add to increase success of blend

Cloves : Money drawing, friendship, stops slander/lies, heat up love, Increase money, luck and happy home, courage, self confidence, strong protection

strengthens psychic shield

Cedar : Strengthen focus, illumination, summons helpful spirit, ward off evil spirits, confidence, perseverance, courage, power

D

Damiana : Attracting love, sex magic, improve sexuality, increase psychic abilities, love spells

Dandelion : Divination, wishes, inviting benevolent spirits

E

Eucalyptus : Healing, attracts and emits healing vibrations, purification, cleansing and soothing

F

Frankincense : Attraction by improving your spiritual connection; attracts abundant love; Magical boost , third eye work, meditation and healing

Five Finger : Heavy on Gaining Favors ,Gambling Luck , Travelers protection, money drawing

G

Galangal : Winning in Court, Doubling Money , Carry for protection, break curses

(Carry to court to make the judge or jury feel favorably inclined to you)

Ginko : memory boosting, focus, clarity , (great as tea or in capsules)

Ginger : Fiery Protection, Gold addition, heats up love, amps up spell/blend

H

Hyssop : Cleansing, purification, lightens vibration, Purge home of evil and negativity

Hibiscus : Lust and love, passionate love, fiery sex, passion promoting

High John the Conqueror Root : Brings great strength and success, personal power, money drawing, conquering, overcoming obstacles

I

Irish Moss : Luck and life flow, gamblers herb, health benefit. Travelers protection herb.

J

Jasmine : Wealth, Divination, abundance drawing, prophetic dreams, soul herb

Jezebel Root : Commanding, bending root, money and achievement, attracting wealthy suitors, attracting better tips for service workers; Getting ones way, also heavy cursing domination root.

K

Kava Kava : Aphrodisiac, divination, visions, astral work , travelers protection (spiritual and physical)

L

Lemongrass : Psychic cleansing, eye opening, refreshing , aura cleansing

Lavender : Love, healing, sleep, restful sleep, peace, healing, works against depression

Lemon Verbana : For a sweet bath, increase attractiveness, prevents bad dreams, increases effectiveness , aura cleansing

M

Marjoram : Great as tea base. Love Spells & Blessings, creates barrier against sadness , restores smiles, optiism Banish grieving, invite benevolent energies

Fights flu and depression

Mugwort : Scrying, lunar magic, protection, lucid dreaming, astral travel , visions (also for tea or smoke blend)

Psychic and very protective, use for long works, protects against fatigue and exhaustion, Nerve calming , wisdom, observation clarity "see what you're seeing"

(not safe for pregnant women)

Myrhh : protection, blessing, purification (heals personal sorrow) Promotes wellness, hex breaking

Mint : energy, money, vitality, customer drawing, prosperity

Mistletoe : Protection for house and children (do not drink) Protects from enemies/evil (best used in sachets and mojo bags)

N

Nettle : hex breaking, uncrossing, protection

Nutmeg : general good luck, luck in gambling, luck drawing, money drawing, can be a light substitute for buckeye, wrap a dollar around nutmeg and carry with you to attract cash

O

Orris Root : Love drawing, making love last, said to make new love and new marriage last for at least seven years.

P

Patchouli : Money and Prosperity, Attracts People, promotes lust , uplifts mood, reduces stress, Aphrodisiac, Enhances Sex Life, Libido, Confidence, Sexuality

Sensuality, Draw love/ money/ Uncrossing , Earthy, Fertility

Palo Santo : Restore the balance of energy in a space , purifying energy clearing and balancing

Penny Royal : healing , evil eye protection, throat chakra work

Q

Queen of the Meadow (Joe Pye / Gravel Root) increases chance of getting a job, altar offering, relieves disharmony on the home, aids in time of distress, happiness, love, divination, inner calm, peace; cheers the heart

R

Rue : (great for spiritual baths) spiritual cleansing, space cleansing

Rosemary : protection, all purpose and can be used as substitute for any herb, blessing , deflects jealousy and gossip

Rose : love

S

Sage : Cleansing, purification, energy clearing

Saffron : wealth, power, recognition , healing love and beauty; rarity.

St Johns Wort : healing dream magic protection, alleviates depression

Skullcap : restful sleep, relaxation, peace, wards off bad dreams

Star Anise : Good Luck, luck in gambling, lucky dreams, ward off envy

Solomon's Seal : Protection, wards off evil spirits, invites benevolent energy

T

Thyme: loyalty, affection, strength thru grief, good luck

V

Verbana : Habit breaking, cleansing, attraction

Vetivert : wealth, love, success, increase power of a spell

Vanilla : Empowering , attract love, sexual drive, powers of the mind

Valerian Root : Ending guilt, negative self talk; Flipping bad situations, Protective,

use in place of graveyard dirt, attach to a woman and men will follow like children

W

Wintergreen : Good fortune and luck , promotes peach in home, protection for children (gambling, fast luck)repels disharmony, negativity and disease*Bless children by bathing so they may always have luck and fortune

Wormwood : increase psychic powers, aid evocation, divination and prophecy , hang in vehicle for protection

Y

Yarrow : Exorcise evil, make love last, happy marriage, clairvoyance

For general substitutions, you may use:
   Rose for any flower
   Rosemary for any herb
   Frankincense for any resin

As with cooking, many herbs may share properties but you must feel, smell and taste which is best for your work or for your blend; Chili powder, Pepper and

Cayenne all bring the heat but what flavor are you looking for? what other herbs are you adding to the mixture, go for "flavor" and build on intention and what goes well together.

Made in the USA
Monee, IL
22 February 2020